THE MATE CODE

N.K. MORGIN

First Edition

Paperback ISBN: 978-0-6457214-0-9
Hardcover ISBN: 978-0-6457214-1-6
eBook-V1.0 ISBN: 978-0-6457214-2-3

deep blue books

Published in 2023 by Deep Blue Books (Melbourne, Australia)
thematecode.com

NATIONAL LIBRARY OF AUSTRALIA

A catalogue record for this
book is available from the
National Library of Australia

THE MATE CODE

Deciphering the Language of Friendship

BY N. K. MORGIN

FOR MY BEST MATES,
MUM & DAD

NIKI SELF PORTRAIT

Hello!

To my new Mate, Friend, Amigo, Pal, Buddy, Chum, Sidekick, Bestie...

Friendship is the greatest gift you can ever give or receive.
A gift that when unwrapped reveals a universal and timeless code -
unspoken gestures of the heart.

The Mate Code is a reminder that it is through our actions
of support, understanding, laughter, and love, that we can
connect to each other.

And it's in these moments that we become mates.

Your new mate, friend, pal..

Niki

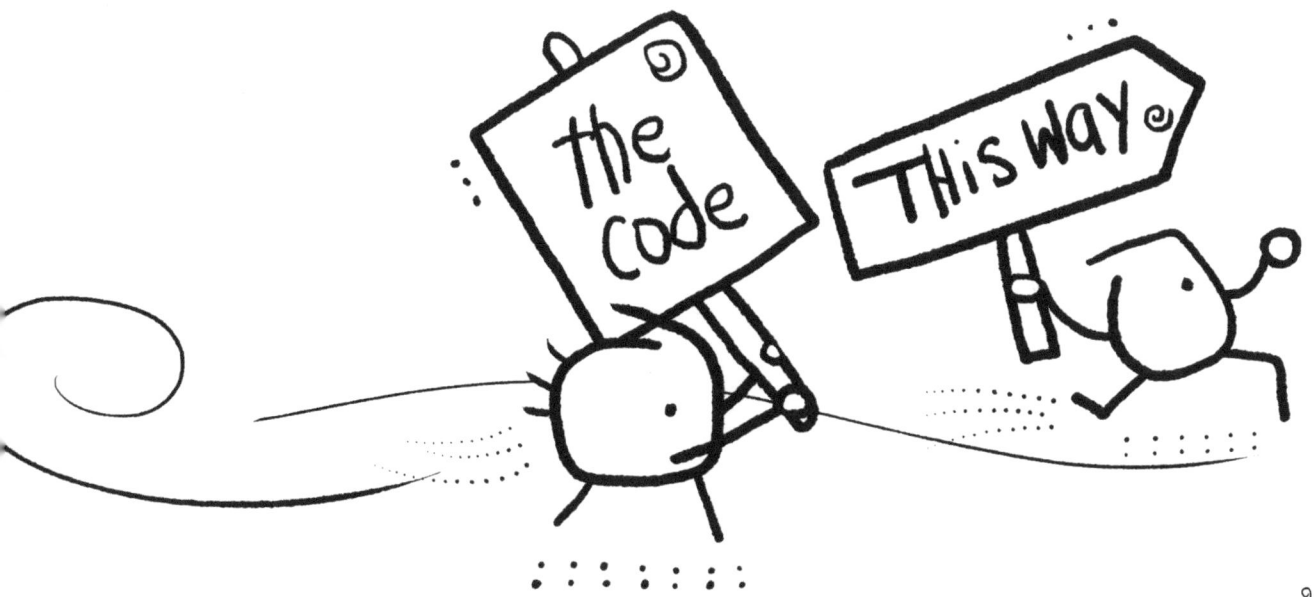

GOOD MATES
SHARE THE LIGHT

ONE GREAT MATE
IS BETTER THAN
100 FOLLOWERS

GREAT MATES
SHARE CAKE

LIFT UP A MATE
WHO CAN'T REACH

A MATE IS AN UMBRELLA
ON A RAINY DAY

BE THE MATE
WHO WILL WAIT 
AT THE FINISH LINE

A GOOD MATE
IS THE FIRST TO ARRIVE
AND THE LAST TO LEAVE

YOUR MATE'S STORIES
BECOME YOURS

BEST MATES SURF
ENDLESS OCEANS

A MATE WHO LAUGHS
AT YOUR JOKES
IS WORTH 1000 SMILES

A MATE TRUE BLUE
STICKS TO YOU
LIKE GLUE

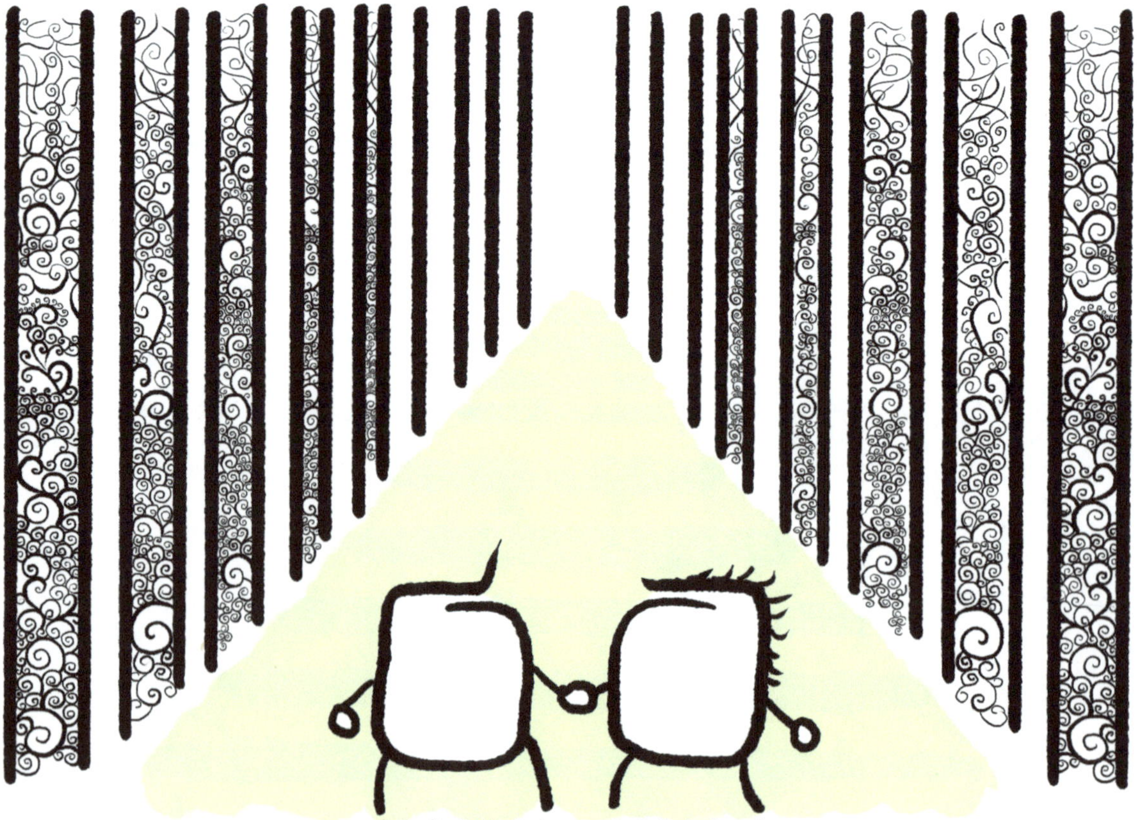

A MATE WILL WALK BESIDE YOU THROUGH THE DARKEST FOREST

GREAT MATES
NEVER MINCE WORDS

A MATE IS
YOUR SPOTTER
NO MATTER HOW HIGH
THE CLIMB

WHEN A MATE
BRINGS YOU APPLES
BAKE THEM A PIE

GOOD MATES
CAN SIT TOGETHER
IN BLISSFUL SILENCE

A MATE,
THE MISSING PIECE,
LIFE'S PUZZLE
NOW COMPLETE

PAINT THE WORLD
WITH KINDNESS,
LET EVERYONE
BE YOUR MATE

YOUR MATESHIP TREE
MAY LOSE SOME LEAVES
SO NEW BUDS 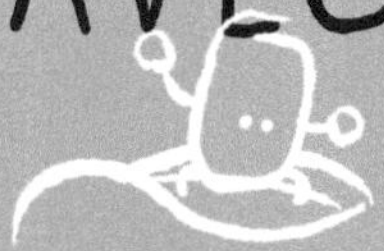
WILL BLOOM STRONGER

NO NAME NEEDED,
A MATE'S HAND EXTENDED,
NEW FRIENDSHIP
COMPREHENDED

GOOD MATES CAN BE
YOUR COMPASS

YOUR DEAREST MATE
WHO KNOWS YOU BEST
LOOKS BACK AT YOU
FROM THE MIRROR

A SOUL MATE
WILL FIND YOU
THROUGH TIME
AND SPACE

OUR GREATEST MATES HAVE FOUR LEGS

GOOD MATES WILL
SHARE THIS BOOK

MATES I'VE SHARED THIS BOOK WITH

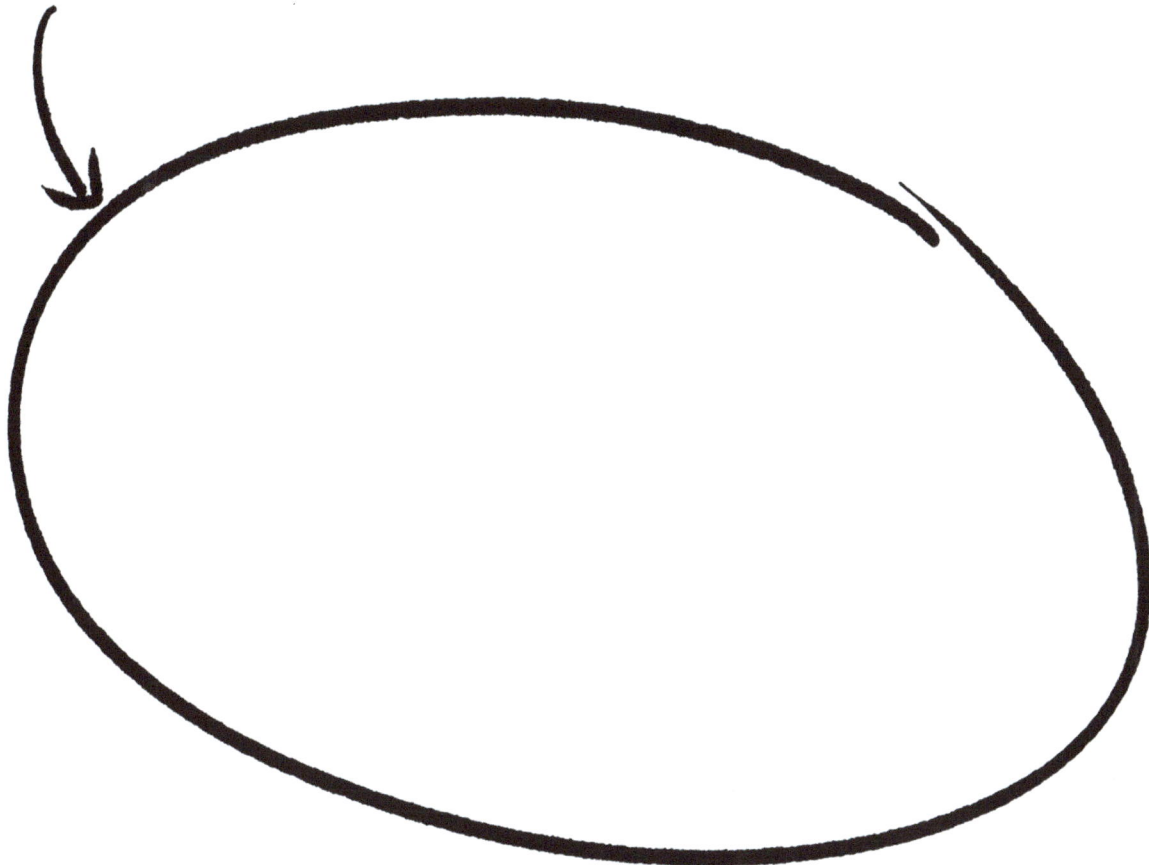

CATCH YA LATER, MATE!

SCAN TO VISIT
THE MATE CODE

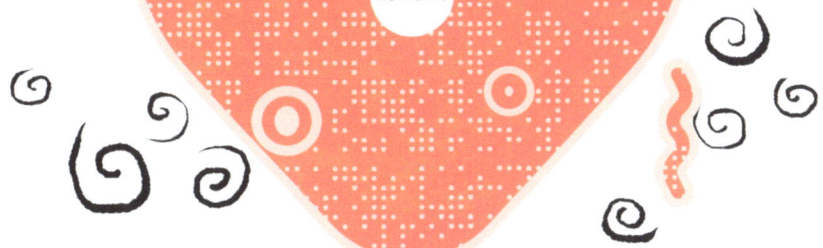

THE MATE CODE

ABOUT THE AUTHOR

Born in Australia last century, N K Morgin is old enough to hoard art supplies, but young enough to remember where she puts them all.

The Mate Code, N K Morgin's debut book, is a retrospective of the friendships that have shaped her life. She'd also like to write and illustrate more books and looks forward to meeting new mates to inspire her.

When not meeting new friends, she enjoys designing and developing games (and has made many for major film and game studios), poking around rock pools for creative inspiration, and buying more art supplies.

Follow her on Instagram @nkmorgin or visit nkmorgin.com

www.ingramcontent.com/pod-product-compliance
Lightning Source LLC
Chambersburg PA
CBHW061138030426
42334CB00004B/88